Faith for the Unbeliever

D1547917

Faith for the Unbeliever

Daniel Chesney Kanter

Skinner House Books
Boston

www.skinnerhouse.org

Printed in the United States

Text and cover design by Suzanne Morgan.
Landscape photo by Daniel Kanter. Window photo by Andrew Neel. Author photo by Stewart Cohen.

print ISBN: 978-1-55896-797-7
eBook ISBN: 978-1-55896-798-4

6 5 4 3 2 1   /   20 19 18 17

Library of Congress Cataloging-in-Publication Data

Names: Kanter, Daniel Chesney, author.
Title: Faith for the unbeliever / Daniel Chesney Kanter.
Description: Boston : Skinner House Books, 2017. | Includes bibliographical
  references. | Description based on print version record and CIP data
  provided by publisher; resource not viewed.
Identifiers: LCCN 2017001832 (print) | LCCN 2017011771 (ebook) | ISBN
  9781558967984 | ISBN 9781558967977 (pbk. : alk. paper)
Subjects: LCSH: Faith. | Religion–Philosophy.
Classification: LCC BL626.3 (ebook) | LCC BL626.3 .K36 2017 (print) | DDC
  202/.2–dc23
LC record available at https://lccn.loc.gov/2017001832

We gratefully acknowledge permission to reprint the following:
"Traveling this high…" and "An autumn wind...," from *The Sound of Water: Haiku by Basho, Buson, Issa and Other Poets*, translated by Sam Hamill, © 1995 by Sam Hamill, reprinted by arrangement with The Permissions Company, Inc., on behalf of Shambhala Publications Inc., Boulder, Colorado, www.shambhala.com; "First Lesson," from *Lifelines: Selected Poems 1950–1999* by Philip Booth, copyright © 1999 by Philip Booth, used by permission of Viking Books, an imprint of Penguin Publishing Group, a division of Penguin Random House LLC, all rights reserved; "To Fill the Void" by Mary Zoll, copyright © 2003 by Mary Zoll, reprinted by permission of author.

❧

Come, thou fount of ev'ry blessing,
tune our hearts to sing thy grace.
Streams of mercy never ceasing,
call for songs of loudest praise.
While the hope of life's perfection
fills our hearts with joy and love,
teach us ever to be faithful,
may we still thy goodness prove.

—Robert Robinson,
    "Come, Thou Fount of Every Blessing"

Contents

Foreword

In an age marked by anxiety and insecurity about our collective future, we see sharp divisions within our global community. They are fueled by racial and ethnic differences, conflicting political ideologies, and diverging visions of what is good for society. But even more significantly, these divides are created by our competing religious belief systems. Amid all our plurality and ambiguity, which so easily lead to conflict and violence, we must ask: How can we forge a meaningful, humane, peaceful, and sustainable way of life for ourselves and our descendants?

Faith for the Unbeliever charts a path in this direction. Making the important distinction between *belief* and *faith*, Daniel Kanter wins our hearts with narratives from his own spiritual journey and also with stories from people who have opened up to him in his role as minister of a large metropolitan Unitarian Universalist congregation.

The "unbeliever" he refers to in the title is not the cynic, not the disaffected one who refuses all forms of belief commitment and leans toward nihilism. Rather, it is the healthy-minded person with common sense, who refuses to be taken in by any absolute claims to this elusive thing called "truth," while at the same time listening and remaining open to anything that appeals to their good sense and reason.

The "unbeliever" may be someone who grew up in a religious community with a strong belief system, but who later rejected that outlook, finding it to be constricting and suffocating. The rejection of previously held beliefs inevitably leaves a vacuum within one's inner being, a gap waiting to be filled by something authentic, liberating, and spiritually satisfying.

The "unbeliever" could also be the person who was not raised with any recognizable or definable religious influence. Precisely because of this, they may begin to ask whether they are missing something, and so feel inspired to launch into an earnest spiritual quest. This person may find themself checking the box marked "spiritual but not religious," joining a group whose numbers seem to be increasing.

The term could even refer to someone who belongs to a particular religious community, attends religious services on a regular basis, and observes the guidelines for behavior as provided by that community, but who remains inwardly dissatisfied and feels an inner thirst for something more spiritually nourishing. Such a person may not be able to take at face value what their religious community upholds or what their church authorities teach, and looks for something deeper. Thus, their heart remains open to listening to and learning from what other religious communities and traditions have to offer in response to life's big questions: Who am I? What am I here for? What am I to do? How can I live my life in a way that will enable me to face my death—whenever and however it comes—with peace and equanimity, with acceptance, and with gratitude for all that I have been given?

When the big, spiritual questions arise for us, we may be able to temporarily brush them aside, considering them to be disruptive or dislocating, as they might distract us from our habitual pursuits of pleasure, possessions, or power. But somehow or other, when the time is ripe, they catch up with us and confront us, stopping us in our tracks. They ask: What is the point of all this?

Taking specific steps to pay attention to the inner voice at the core of our being, and to live in accordance with its promptings, is to take up a form of spiritual practice. To start this process, we need to see things with a clear eye, and find freedom and resolve to set our life in order, and thus be enabled to hear those promptings from within.

This small book helps us get started, by considering faith as a fourfold set of lenses that enables us to see the "deep down things," in the words of poet Gerard Manley Hopkins. Daniel Kanter shares precious nuggets from his own journey, one that, with all its contours, constantly moves him to "respond to the callings and urgings of the deepest places of my spirit." He invites us, his readers, to take this kind of inner journey as well and, led on by faith, to respond to these callings and urgings from the depths of our own being.

Ruben L. F. Habito
Professor of World Religions and Spirituality,
Perkins School of Theology
Guiding Teacher, Maria Kannon Zen Center, Dallas, Texas

Introduction

> The road to self-knowledge does not pass through
> faith. But only through the insight we gain by pur-
> suing the fleeting light in the depth of our being do
> we reach the point where we can grasp what faith is.
> How many have been driven into outer darkness by
> empty talk about faith as something to be rationally
> comprehended, something "true."
>
> —Dag Hammarskjöld

We have been sold a bill of goods when it comes to faith.
We have been told we either have it or we don't. After some
careful thinking on this, I believe that is completely wrong.
We all have faith, but we rarely define it in ways that can
help us. We have given over this concept, like so many others, to someone else, even though it is right in the midst of
everything we do. The faith I'm talking about is an essential
part of our daily lives, and if we look below the surface it
can ground us in ways that many of us haven't yet explored.

Many of us don't begin this exploration because we're told that faith is about belief statements. Yet a nontraditional faith can pave the way to new beginnings.

What is faith? When we get right down to it, it's pretty clear we don't know. But it's often taken to mean strong religious feelings, or a devout belief in something unprovable. If the only people who had faith were those who devoutly believed in unprovable religious concepts, many of us would be left out of the conversation. To go beyond these superficial definitions, we must move past purely traditional religious ideas and consider things that we practice every day but that are rarely given much attention.

It has been my great privilege to spend the last eight years serving as the senior minister of a large Unitarian Universalist congregation in Dallas, Texas. I came to this profession out of my own longing to explore the ways of the spirit. I actually never thought I would be a minister. I have been an apple farmer and a teacher. But during my early adulthood I found myself pursuing religion in classrooms and in person. I was drawn to serve others to make a difference rather than a dollar. I was comfortable in religious settings, whether Hindu temples in South India or the Jewish temple my great-grandparents helped start in the Berkshires. I was told by a minister from my childhood that I might pursue the ministry, but I shrugged off his suggestion. I went on my wild path, only to be eventually drawn back, like Jonah, to do the thing

I felt called to do: return home and serve. After teaching in a public school program in Burlington, Vermont, for youth who were one step from prison, I went to seminary, and from there to serving King's Chapel in Boston. There I was, a Unitarian Universalist Buddhist Jew serving a Christian Unitarian church, when I got a call from Texas asking me to consider a position covering for a minister who was going on sabbatical. I was comfortable in my nice office on Beacon Street, with a small yet complicated congregation. And all I knew about Texas was it had Longhorn cattle and cactus!

I was wrong about so many things. I was wrong that being comfortable is always the right way to go. I was wrong about what I could do as a minister. And I was wrong about Texas—or at least I was wrong about Dallas, which had no Longhorns (except the graduates of the University of Texas, who wore jackets and ties to church) and no cactus to speak of! I told the Dallas congregation that I'd give them nine months, and dragged my reluctant family (including a one-year-old child) south. I ended up staying sixteen years. I have had four jobs in the church in Dallas, and now serve as its CEO and senior minister.

My ministry has given me a front-row seat as a witness to the faith lives of hundreds of people making their way through life as best they can. I often ask my parishioners to describe their faith. Many times they begin by describing what they believe—or don't believe. But as they continue, something remarkable starts to happen: They begin to describe ways that they are faithful. They tell stories from their lives. Stories about trust and about loyalty. Stories that illustrate their unique view of the world. And, yes, stories about beliefs—but beliefs born out of their struggles to make meaning of their lives. Their stories often fill in the blanks of a generic definition of faith and show how faith can be more than the proclamations of a long-ago prophet or words found in ancient scriptures.

After walking with folks in their faith journeys, and wrestling with these questions myself, I have come to realize that we have an opportunity to redefine faith and make it part of the foundation of a great variety of spiritual and religious ways of living. When we deliberately engage with and even practice these aspects of faith, life becomes more meaningful and purposeful.

More than an adherence to a belief system, faith is an orientation to life. It is looking out at the world from a particular perspective, and using that perspective to consider the meaning of our existence.

I have identified four areas in which we may look for a faithful approach to life: our guiding beliefs, areas of trust, loyalties, and worldview. I think of them as like four panes of a window. We look out through them, and on the other side is the vast landscape of experience. One pane may need a little cleaning, while another may be more clear.

This book is organized to address each of these ways to look at faith and asks you, the reader, to reflect on how you might see yourself as a person of faith without the traditional and, frankly, flat definitions of that word. It explores what it means to live by beliefs and the limits of the concept of belief. It engages with the concept of trusting in the world as a way of nurturing a sense of groundedness and presence. Fidelity, or loyalty, gets its own chapter, exploring what it means to be loyal to decisions or people and the benefits and challenges that arise from doing so. The book then turns to the concept of worldview and discusses how we hold a vision of the world that we may or may not be aware of, and how we can learn to develop alternative visions. Finally, the book asks you to synthesize your responses to these four aspects of faith and to see what your faith looks like.

At the end of each chapter you will find reflection questions to consider. These are meant to help you delve deeper into each of the four aspects of faith. The queries may serve you well as writing prompts for personal journaling, or you might discuss them with a friend who is also reading this book. Moving slowly and intentionally through the text will help you reflect more deeply on how these ideas apply to your faith life, which is the only true point.

To some extent, everyone has examined what they believe, who or what they trust in, what they are loyal to, and how they see the world. To make that examination more intentional, we can listen to and tell stories that point toward ways to consider the poignant moments of our lives. Treat the stories in this book—some of which come from my travel adventures—as metaphors or myths that can add depth or perspective to your own search. See if you can find in them truths that make sense in a broader context. Both seeking out adventure and thinking spiritually deepen the everyday experiences and the great adventures of life. We can have adventures of the soul while standing at the kitchen sink, gazing out the window at our suburban neighborhood, or while sitting in church. They can happen on top of mountains or while peering at mountains of papers we need to file. Realizing the ways that faith and life converge in the heart while walking hand in hand with a child up the preschool steps on the first day of school is a kind of faith adventure. But it is only a faith adventure if we consider it deliberately.

I see these awakenings in my parishioners all the time. Sometimes they come easily, and sometimes we need to be jarred awake to see the truth of what is happening within and around us. Sometimes that means traveling to the edge of the world, and sometimes it means waking up while doing the dishes.

Walking with people through the highs and lows of their spiritual lives, I have come to realize that almost every experience can be food for the soul. To transform an old phrase, we might say that an examined life leads to a richer experience and a more deliberate existence. We can live a better life by passing our experiences through the fire of the heart as a way to understand the inner landscape of who we are and the unique contributions we make to the world. If approached with self-awareness, thought, and the ability to step back far enough to see them in perspective, all our day-to-day moments can be food for the soul.

I hope that this book will stimulate you to examine what you know about faith and how you might transform it from belief statements to orientations. This reclamation project takes some work. It requires you to ask what "adventures" you are taking and what kind of path you are on. And now, let's take some journeys together as we begin our exploration.

Belief

Wise fool stories are told for entertainment and teaching around the world. In Turkey, they often involve a man named Hodja. One day Hodja is working in his garden when a friend comes to see him. His friend sees that Hodja is putting bread crumbs in his garden and asks, "Hodja, why are you putting bread crumbs in your garden?" Hodja replies, "To keep the tigers away!" His friend laughs and says, "Hodja, there aren't any tigers for miles around." Hodja looks at his friend and says, "See, it works!"

Sometimes there is no arguing with people who have strong beliefs. The kind of belief that Hodja displays in this story, confident that he is right because he refuses to see evidence against him, borders on superstition. The story is amusing, but the lesson can appear in more serious forms. I meet people all the time who buy a belief wholesale and refuse to adapt it to their surroundings. I find it hard to understand people who don't believe in evolution, global climate change, or other scientifically proven and observable facts. Of course, the picture is murkier when dealing with religious or spiritual beliefs. When we enter into conversations about the efficacy of prayer or life after death we are on a new playing field, where there are many personal experiences but little proof. It is easy for some of us to plant our feet and make statements of unwavering belief. For others, it's not that easy. But none of us can negotiate the world without some beliefs. Beliefs are guideposts for decision making. They help us know what we are doing and why.

I know people who say their beliefs change every day. I know people who say they believe in nothing at all. One member of my church told me that he knows that atheism doesn't exist because one can't "believe in nothing." We all have beliefs, whether they are religious or not. And they probably shift as we mature and change. Beliefs are foundations and supports in our lives, and they may range widely—we may believe in God as savior or in sustainable agriculture. But we spend a lot of time defending our beliefs, like sentries trying to defend a castle, without reflecting on how they can serve us or hinder us. To base our faith on belief alone is to teeter on the edge of a spiritual abyss. And if we challenge our firmly guarded belief systems, we may be surprised by what we discover and the adventures we enter into.

Faith and belief are often considered the same thing. In some contexts, having a religious belief is defined as "having faith." In religious terms, belief is conventionally understood as assent. It often comes up in conversation in phrases like "What I believe is . . . " Such phrases raise questions for us: Do I believe in God? Do I believe in some force that guides me? Do my beliefs sustain me as a spiritual person? In this book, having a religious belief is considered to be only one way of having faith, but there are others as well. Ken Wilbur, a philosopher and writer, says, "Belief is the lowest form of religious involvement, and, in fact, it often seems to operate with no authentic religious connection whatsoever."

The word *believe* has changed meaning over time in significant ways. It originally meant "to hold dear," essentially, "to love." The pre-modern understanding of belief thus had a relational quality, implying an attitude toward or relationship with a person or God. The modern and secular use of *believe* often involves arguments over whether things are real or not. In recent times we have come to speak of "belief systems": sets of presuppositions, or conceptual frameworks, through which we view the world. As a result, a broken belief leaves us with only pieces of what we once thought was true. But if we return to the pre-modern understanding of believing as setting the heart upon something, the air clears. Instead of pinning our belief on the absolute truth of something, we might set our heart upon completing something like a journey. Of course, if the journey goes wrong, our heart might still break.

History provides innumerable examples of how beliefs have changed and, in turn, changed lives. George de Benneville, who was born in London in 1703 and sent to sea as a boy, tells such a story. One day on the ship he served, he encountered some "Moors" on the deck. As a white Christian, de Benneville held these men in contempt, until he had an exchange with them that created a dramatic shift in his beliefs. In *The Life and Trance of George de Benneville*, he writes,

When [I] arrived at the age of twelve years, I was very wild [and] believed myself to be of a different mass from mankind in general, and by this fond imagination I was self-exalted, and believed myself to be more than other men. But God soon convinced me to the contrary.

As it was designed that I should learn navigation, I was sent to sea in a vessel of war belonging to a little fleet bound to the coast of Barbary with presents, and to renew the peace with Algiers, Tunis, and Tripolis. Being arrived at Algiers, as I walked upon deck I saw some Moors who brought some refreshments to sell. One of them slipped down and tore a piece out of one of his legs. Two of his companions, having lain him on the deck, each of them kissed the wound, shedding tears upon it, then turned towards the rising of the sun, they cried in such a manner that I was much moved with anger at their making such a noise and ordered my waiter to bring them before me. Upon demanding the reason of their noise, they perceived that I was angry, asked my pardon, and told me the cause was owing to one of their brothers having hurt his leg by a fall and that they kissed the wound in order to sympathize with him, and likewise shed tears upon it and took part with him; and as tears were saltish, they [were] a good remedy to heal the same; and the reason of their turning towards the sun's rising was to invoke him who created the sun to have compassion upon their poor brother, and prayed he would please to heal him. Upon that I was so convinced, and moved within, that I thought my heart would break, and that my life was about to leave me. My eyes were filled with tears, and I felt such an internal condemnation, that I was obliged to cry out and say, "Are these Heathens? No; I confess before God they are Christians, and I myself am a Heathen!" Behold the first conviction that the grace of our Sovereign Good employed: he was pleased to convince a white person by blacks! One who carried the name of a Christian by a pagan, and who was obliged to confess himself but a heathen.

Waking from his beliefs and prejudice, de Benneville confesses that his heart breaks and he is changed. The change in his beliefs about these men opened a world for him and set him on the path toward a lifelong commitment to preach the universal love of God for all people. He was a pioneer in trying to change people's beliefs about those they didn't understand and characterized as less than human.

Can beliefs change? Of course. What does it take to change our beliefs? Sometimes it takes a lot. Being open to those changes is part of living out a flexible faith.

When dealing with belief, we will inevitably encounter the challenge of doubt. While some religious dogma shuns doubt, it can be a useful device in the toolbox of our faith. Martin Luther, the sixteenth-century reformer of the Catholic Church and founder of the Lutheran religion, famously said, "What is more miserable than uncertainty?" He was challenging the great Erasmus of Rotterdam, who had declared that he would rather go over at once to the camp of the skeptics, if the authority of Scripture and the Church would permit him to do so. This rejection of doubt stands in contrast to the Buddhist teaching "If you meet the Buddha on the road, kill him," which is understood to mean that if you think you have the answers to big spiritual questions, think again. Unlike Luther, Buddhists freely admit that to concretize our beliefs is to stand in heresy, and hinders our development. To doubt is to seek. Once we take on a topic such as doubt and let it sink in, it can affect our whole life.

Doubt is both amazing and subtle. It is a way of seeing the world that takes for granted that there are no easy answers. Some people may find doubt the most satisfying base on which to ground a worldview. John Shanley's play *Doubt: A Parable* contains a number of lines of dialogue that ring out for those of us who see faith as inclusive of doubt. For example, one character claims, "Certainty is an emotion, not a fact." The four characters in the play represent four positions on a spectrum from certainty to doubt. One character is steadfastly certain until doubt cracks through the hardened walls of her heart. One is wracked with self-doubt and easily persuaded by another. The third is living in the paradox of faith and doubt and trying his best to do what is right, although he may hold a secret that could destroy him. And the last character represents unconditional love in her unwavering loyalty to her son; she is the playwright's antidote to the dilemma. Shanley has his main character Father Flynn say, "Doubt can be a bond as powerful and sustaining as certainty. When you are lost, you are not alone."

Doubt has its usefulness, but it can also cast us into a spiral of questioning and confusion. The Unitarian Universalist Association once took out ads in *Time Magazine* that proclaimed, "When in doubt, pray. When in prayer, doubt." That started me thinking about the benefits and perils of doubt itself.

We all know people who lack a healthy dose of doubt. Some people know they are right, they know God is with and for them, they know they are going to heaven, and they might even say that they know certain others aren't. Some of them read the Gospels literally and maintain, as Jesus says in the Gospel of John (20:29), "Blessed are those who have not seen and yet have come to believe."

Like the apostle Thomas, whom Jesus was gently scolding with those words, we may refuse to believe things we cannot see and touch. A dear friend of my wife took her own life in Spain, and we never saw the place where she did it, never touched the body, never read the note she left behind, never saw any of the scene with our eyes. We only heard the story as we were told it by her family. Our first reaction was total disbelief. This couldn't have happened, it didn't, it hasn't. And to this day, some of her family and friends deny that she ended her own life. She might have slipped, they say, might have made a mistake.

Indeed, we sometimes deny even what we can see. In a world of computer images and films created on green screens, we are often challenged to determine what is real and what is not.

Doubt helps deepen who we are. When we doubt something, we can have one of two responses: to dispel it or to get curious about it. The most curious people are the ones who learn the most. A member of my church whom I memorialized years ago was always curious, wanting to learn, wanting to be deepened, and unwilling to take something on another person's word. Her curiosity and refusal to settle for hearsay moved her to write five volumes on American artists and create a reference book on American art more than three thousand pages long. Doubt is a seed that keeps us from settling for another's truth. It is also, in a strange way, the first growth of a deep faith, a sign that faith is alive and ready to grow. Doubt is nothing less than an opportunity to re-enter and examine the present.

On the other hand, the perils of doubt are also recognizable: insecurity, perpetual anxiety, and lack of trust. Doubt doesn't help much when something in your life is going terribly wrong or has been smothered in you. But certainty might not help either. When I care for people in my church who need a listening ear, I try to remain with them in the mystery of their pain, to help them not turn away, to hold them in love, but I rarely tell them that it will all work out for the best.

One day a middle-aged member of my church came to talk with me. We had enjoyed polite banter before, but never a moment so serious. She had been forced out of her job as a school official. At first I didn't understand why she had lost her job. I listened, waiting for her story to emerge, and she gradually revealed that she had been pushed out because of politics and maybe a little racism and possibly even sexism. Then she hit the emotional core and burst into tears. What brought her all this way to sit in my office and tell me her long story were two painful aspects of losing her job. First, she loved the children in that school and had been removed so forcefully that she had had no chance to say goodbye. Second, and more poignant, she was embarrassed at losing a job everyone knew she loved, seeing her dismissal as a personal failure and a public humiliation.

I couldn't tell her it would all be okay, because I can't read the future. But I told her that her community loved her and that her students knew that she loved them. I told her that facing the pain of humiliation was going to be hard, but we could do it together. Once we both stopped crying, she left feeling like she could face the world. The support I gave her isn't magic — it's a belief in each other that we can learn to share, and it's making space for confession. She doubted her future, but she could hold on — and she would, until she could see more clearly and move ahead with dignity restored.

Life is a mystery, and we are disingenuous when we deny this by predicting the future for those in pain.

One way to entertain doubt is to hold the paradox of faith and doubt in dynamic balance. We should not let absolutes grab hold of us. This seems like a dangerous gamble. If we are too doubtful we may end up in the place Shanley described in the preface to his play, "a place where we know that we don't know . . . anything." Sometimes I feel that way. But I think deep down we do know something. To give up on knowing is to close our eyes and turn away from what is right in front of us.

Once, I was at a retreat in East Texas, among the piney woods, studying silence and spirituality, when someone played a piece of music by Bobby McFerrin. It was a rewriting of the twenty-third psalm. Near the end, it exalted the divine Mother and Daughter and the "Holy of Holies," before concluding with the words,

> As it was in the beginning, is now and ever shall be,
> World without end. Amen.

Just as the amen was sung, a bird in the distance called out, and I thought, there it is, yes. We know something deep and abiding about life: As it was in the beginning, it is now and ever shall be, world without end. We know, if we are honest, that life goes on, even through the shipwrecks, even through despair and loss. In some way it's comforting that we aren't the culmination of life; the earth will live when the human noise ceases. Theologian Paul Tillich writes, in *The New Being*, "We may not grasp anything in the depth of our uncertainty, but that we are grasped by something ultimate, which keeps us in its grasp and from which we may strive in vain to escape, remains absolutely certain."

Life is miracle. In the end we might have to carefully balance the poles of faith and doubt and be willing to be grasped by something ultimate. What we have we can't take for granted. Writers and musicians of all times have reminded us that even in the darkest hour we have to open our eyes and see what life holds in all its beautiful catastrophes. And our job is to do our best to hold gently the strands of certainty and uncertainty, faith and doubt, which pull us in directions we might not expect. The trick is to walk the middle path and not pull too hard on either one, so we can see what is in front of our eyes honestly and confidently. To walk the middle path means to believe in things that are true enough, but to maintain an eternal "maybe, maybe not" as we pass through life's experiences, open to the possibility that we are wrong.

My long journey to reclaim the Unitarian Universalist tradition of my upbringing started with questions about faith. For me, the questions themselves were lanterns in the dark. They asked: Does my faith change my life for the better? What God do I believe in? And: Can I be a person of faith without believing in a supreme being? When we allow faith to be defined solely as "belief," who we are does not link in a satisfying way to how we are in the world. Such a definition is unworkable in a culture that seeks meaning in the context of twenty-first-century science and technology and the mingling of ideas and cultures from all over the globe. If we understand faith only as "belief," we have lost the battle to those who maintain that we cannot be people of faith unless we subscribe to a traditional religious system. If we allow faith to remain outside of the realm of what we can understand or experience, we may miss out on the richness of seeing it in our everyday experience.

In contemporary society, the continual advancement of scientific discoveries, the wide variety of religious perspectives, and the increase in multi-faith interactions all combine to offer us an opportunity to open up to new ways of conceiving of faith. Whether we take that opportunity is up to us.

Reflection Questions

❧ What do you believe is true for you? How do you know these things? What do you base these beliefs on?

❧ If you were talking to the wisest, most trustworthy sage in the world, do you think that person might let you hold on to those beliefs, or would that person challenge them?

❧ What is a belief that once worked for you but doesn't any longer? Can you discard it?

❧ What do you doubt?

Trust

Who and what can you trust? You might be a person who easily trusts others, or one who begins with suspicion. Most of us fall into one category or the other. Trust is an ingredient of faith that sometimes challenges us to give up some control, or the notion that we are in control. It means finding comfort in change. Sharon Salzberg, an American Buddhist writer, points out that "faith as trust" is confidence in change. Salzberg often encourages her followers to see faith as a way toward action and commitment. Living at ease and trusting in the world can create a sense of groundedness and presence. Faith is what gets us moving in the morning or enables us to take on new challenges, because every day in some way we move toward the unknown circumstances that will greet us.

But fear can challenge this kind of mindset. American culture plays on many fears and can make it difficult to live with a strong sense of trust in the world. Many of us are taught from an early age, both implicitly and directly, that we cannot trust others. Sensationalized news stories teach that the only safe way is to fear the stranger and protect what we have at all costs. With this mindset we can forget how much good there is in our world. The answer isn't to let ourselves become isolated. Study after study shows that social cohesion is good for us, for our happiness and our health. And just as friends can increase our happiness, isolation can increase our desire for self-protection.

I don't suggest that we trust everyone and see the silver lining in everything. But if we imagine that the world is always untrustworthy, our soul will suffer for it. If we hear that life is only pain and suffering, we may be crippled by fear. I remember how I carried distrust in my shoulders when I visited New York City as a teenager. I lived across the George Washington Bridge in New Jersey and went into the city often, sometimes on my own. But I felt I always had to put on my "armor" to go to the big city, because I couldn't trust anyone. As I look back at that time in my life, I realize how damaging it was to fear my surroundings, how detrimental to my sense of well-being. While my wariness probably saved my neck a few times, it took me a lifetime to recover from that ingrained wariness. To this day my friends tell me I'm paranoid about someone stealing my bicycle or something in my car. I am almost obsessive about locking things up and protecting my valuables. The habit of distrust can get in the way of living fully. To counter that and begin to trust a person is a great gift to the world and to ourselves.

This form of faith is not trusting in a set of statements about something, someone, or some God. It is trusting something, someone, or some God. The Unitarian poet Philip Booth described trust in the buoyancy of life in his poem "First Lesson." In it he describes the first swimming lesson he gave his daughter, in the waters of coastal Maine.

Lie back, daughter, let your head
be tipped back in the cup of my hand.
Gently, and I will hold you. Spread
your arms wide, lie out on the stream
and look high at the gulls. A dead-
man's-float is face down. You will dive
and swim soon enough where this tidewater
ebbs to the sea. Daughter, believe
me, when you tire on the long thrash
to your island, lie up, and survive.
As you float now, where I held you
and let go, remember when fear
cramps your heart what I told you:
lie gently and wide to the light-year
stars, lie back, and the sea will hold you.

To learn to fully trust is to learn to give ourselves completely into another's care. The opportunity to "lie back" in the hands of another in the sea of life and practice trusting them can be a great privilege. This kind of trust can be life altering. The kind of faith described in "First Lesson" points to a willingness to be held by a person or an unseen force in the mystery of being. It's a good invitation to take a risk and let go of control.

I used this poem as a reading in a service one Sunday, and afterward a member of the congregation approached me and asked, "Do you remember that feeling of putting yourself in another's arms?" I wasn't sure where he was going with that until he went on,

I learned to swim when I was forty-five years old. I was terrified of the water. My sister had drowned when I was young, and we didn't spend time on or around the water. But I realized I had to face that fear and learn. And I realized what I was doing was learning to trust again. For forty-four years of my life I distrusted the very thing that flows through all of us, water. When I learned to rest in it my life changed, and not only could I do the breaststroke, but I could trust other people, believe in them, and surrender a piece of myself to every relationship I have.

When I had caught my breath I thanked him for that story and wished him well. "I trust you," he said as he walked off. Risk sometimes requires that we go a few metaphorical miles from home, beyond the borders of comfort, and its rewards can present new opportunities to learn and build on faith.

In 1987, my friend Vijay and I took a bicycle trip through rural southern India. We passed through villages that had no hotels or restaurants, and after a few days the bread we had brought from home molded and soured. We "relied on the kindness of strangers," to quote the playwright. One evening it was getting late and we couldn't find a place to stop. We eventually followed train tracks to an outdoor station. We were exhausted when we arrived, so we set down our things and laid our bodies on a bench a hundred yards away. We could see the stationmaster at a distance, closing up for the night, but we figured he couldn't see us, and that even if he did he would not be bothered by two sleeping travelers. It's common to see whole families sleeping on train station floors in India, covered like corpses with cloth while they wait for the morning train.

Everything seemed fine until the annoyed stationmaster woke us up with a prod from his baton and told us to follow him. His large handlebar mustache, thick arms, and pressed white uniform conveyed more than his words did. Still trying to wake up enough to understand just what was happening, we obeyed, knowing that we were at the mercy of his authority. He walked us to a shed behind the station and pointed to the floor, on which were piled mats and supplies for the station, sacks of rice and tea, and crates of clay teacups. Then he showed us into what appeared to our weary eyes to be a holding cell equipped with bars on the windows. When he left, he took our bikes and locked the door.

We were too tired to discuss what this imprisonment meant, but I will never forget the sound of the lock turning on that heavy wooden door. The only thought I had before sleep overwhelmed me was: What would a stationmaster in a remote rural train station do with prisoners? We figured he might put us on a train to the next city to be prosecuted for trespassing, or deal with us himself in the morning. We slept deeply, but uneasily.

The stationmaster returned the next morning, unlocking the door and stepping into the crammed quarters. We feared what might come next, since he was larger than both of us put together and took up half the room. And then a surprising thing happened; a small woman in a colorful sari stepped from behind him and put in front of us two plates of idlis, steamed rice flour dumplings often eaten with coconut chutney for breakfast in the south, and a tray with a pot of hot chai and the same cups that we saw in the crates around us. I realized much later that this woman was his wife and had put on her best sari to serve us that morning.

We sat with this official and his wife, eating well and telling them of our adventures. We weren't prisoners after all. We were being kept safe from anyone who might have followed us along the tracks, and from the thieves who regularly stole from the station. After a morning of stories and laughter, they showed us to our bikes, which had been carefully stored in the station control room, and sent us off with our bags filled with food. Our hearts were more relieved than full, but we were happy to have been so carefully sheltered by our new friends.

I have asked myself many times why we mistrusted this man. Perhaps, despite his good intentions, we saw only his unquestionable authority, and assumed the worst. But did we do so because of the situation, or because of something inherent in us?

While I was in India, I also studied with a Brahmin priest near the Meenakshi Temple in Madurai. He often talked about risk, and he told me that the Hindu philosophy of Vedanta teaches that to risk is to create a spiritual life "on the razor's edge." To risk is to step out past our comfort zones, to know that we could lose everything we guard about who we are, and to go anyway, because the reward might be a valuable change. The reward is gained by surrendering to something greater than solitary existence. And in reaching for the possibilities that the world offers, we often find a strength of heart and soul that we did not know we had.

I do not mean that we all have to get on bicycles and climb mountains to do any of this. Many people risk something every day just by getting out of bed and engaging with the world. So to analyze risk and surrender and understand how they function in life is to touch on a kind of faith that can strengthen. Even trying something new, or having a conversation with a neighbor, can be a journey that puts us in a position to take a risk. *Risk* is a relative term—what one person finds perfectly safe and familiar may be a razor's edge for another.

Our goal is to gain a deeper sense of existential comfort and to combat a cynical view of the world. We risk a lot when we give ourselves over to another's love or care. I have met a lot of people who can't do that, because they have been hurt by the shattering of previous relationships, and still bear the wounds and scars. I have met people who were abused as children and who now can't trust enough to have a partner in their lives. Sometimes things like this, that we didn't cause, fray the fabric of our trust, and I respect that. To trust another can be a perilous business, especially when there are some who can't return trust or are reckless with the lives around them. But the strongest thing in the world may be the trust that is born of another's love and care. The psychologist Erik Erikson held that trust that grows from the care of a loving parent is the basis of all faith practices. If we lack love and care in our early years, that lack can cause us to distrust each other deeply and thus, in his paradigm, mistrust God. I think he is right, but I also believe that trust can be strengthened like a muscle if we can face the past with courage and transform hurt into wholeness.

Trust, then, on the "razor's edge," means risking enough that we do not lose our balance. This balance is tricky to find, but we will probably never find it if we never step out of our comfort zone. Its opposite, I think, is a life of suspicion or anxiety. The Bible repeatedly admonishes us against such a failure in faith, with angels, prophets, and even Jesus telling us "Fear not" and "Do not be anxious." When angels appear to biblical characters, including Mary, often the first words they say are "Fear not," and Jesus repeats the reassurance. The story of Jesus I love most is the one in which he sends his disciples out on a boat into a lake and then walks out across the water's surface toward them (Mark 6:47–50). They are terrified, thinking they see a ghost or demon, but he calms them, saying, "Take courage! It is I. Don't be afraid." Then he climbs into the boat with them, and the wind dies down. And they are completely amazed.

One measure of trust in our lives is the amount of anxiety we carry. We all carry different amounts, but most of us can identify moments when we feel more anxious about decisions or the presence of certain people in our lives. Some of our anxiety is justified. Trusting someone who doesn't return that trust or repeatedly breaks it is a bad idea. As with most things, but maybe especially with trust, we have to be wise as serpents and gentle as doves. This is a challenge. I freely admit that some people don't deserve trust. But when we catch ourselves mistrusting our close friends or family or teachers because of our own anxiety, we should realize that we may have some work to do. Sometimes we have to take Jesus' advice and calm ourselves, and sometimes we have to trust our intuition and not get in a car with a stranger we have a bad feeling about, or let someone into our lives who we sense will be destructive. We can't always make the best decisions, and many things are out of our control. The antidote to anxiety isn't a life permanently on the razor's edge, but sometimes taking a leap into unknown space helps us combat it, helps us practice trusting that we will land somewhere safe.

Before I set off from Texas on a solo cross-country bicycle trip, those who cared for my safety told me that the world is full of crazy people. I responded that I appreciated their concern for me and cherished it deeply. And I assured my advisors that my faith holds that people are essentially good and that that belief, however naïve, would comfort me through any difficult encounters with the crazy ones. I believed that I could count on the virtue and mercy of many and forge a connection to those I did not know because I trusted in the world. And I found that I was right most of the time.

I know it is easier for me than for many others to trust the world I threw myself into, because I have never been taught, by abuse or other painful experiences, to distrust others. I have certainly had my heart broken and the rug pulled out from under me from time to time, so I know something about the failure of trust. I also know many who have made the long journey back from the damage others have done to them. I have seen people overcome their own great distrust by deciding to take risks again, or to take the hand of someone who would lead them to a stronger place within them. One parishioner told me that she had been raped in college by a man who broke into her dorm room through a window one night. It took her many years to examine and transform the horror she experienced. With the help of a loving partner she learned to trust that she could be intimate with another again, and when she told me this story she said that her strongest emotion now about that event in her life was compassion for the man who raped her. I was taken aback by this statement. I understood her moving on after many years of learning to trust again, but I was surprised by her saying that she felt sadness for the man, almost empathy for his struggle. I thought that the level of trust she had attained was like a black belt in karate, because she had transformed pain and loss and a broken trust into something much deeper through her care for the person who violated her. I don't know if I could do the same. She said to me, "I suffered, and I know that suffering was because that man was suffering. I never knew who he was, but I have compassion, not hate, for him." This kind of spiritual response is rare, especially to such extreme violations, but it's the kind of spiritual response that some people can achieve. Admittedly some of us have bigger mountains to climb.

There were only a few moments on my cycling trip when I truly feared for my safety, and they were far outweighed by the welcome and care I received from the people I met. I remember one day my alarm bell began to ring. I was in Owensboro, Kentucky, a culture foreign to this Yankee, and moreover I was in the heart of meth-lab country. I had arranged to stay with a man I will call Hank, whom I knew only through a couch-surfing website for bicycle travelers. I was having a rough day; the busy road had only a six-inch shoulder and a rumble strip to protect me against cars swerving and forcing me off the road. Also, I had a heavy headwind. I called Hank, and he said that no one he knew rode bicycles on that road, and that he was fishing nearby and would come pick me up. An hour later he pulled up in a jeep, with his fishing boat hitched to the back and his Jack Russell in the window. As he got out of the jeep I saw him put a pistol on the seat. The sight of the pistol was a surprise to me and set me thinking fast about an escape route.

Hank helped me tie the bike into his boat, and we took off. As we drove, he asked me what I did, and I told him I was a minister. I could see him give a sigh of relief. Then I asked him about the pistol, and he said that with all the meth production around, he had to be careful when out in the country. I had the sense he also meant that I could have been setting up an ambush, and the pistol was meant to protect him from me.

Hank and I had a great visit, talking about bluegrass music (which was born in that area), cycling, and the world. I realized that Hank's life had been filled with experiences that challenged his trust in people and the world. He had grown up in a bar owned by his father. He had seen a lot of abusive behavior by adults there, and had probably borne the brunt of some himself. He told me he rarely drank because of what he had seen as a child, and how his way out of that place had been to become a drummer and excel in music even as a teenager. He was safer behind the trap set than anywhere else. He had always struggled with fitness, and now often rode a bicycle as well as trained indoors in the winter. I think he took in bicycle travelers as a way to build up his trust and confidence in those around him. He also had a fully equipped touring bicycle in his home office, ready to go. When I asked him when he was going to tour, he told me his hope was to go cross-country, from Virginia to Oregon, sometime in the next seven years. I encouraged him to start sooner, but I thought that it might take that long for him to build up enough trust to be as vulnerable as I was out on the road. For Hank, life was a series of small changes. He wasn't ready to pack up, close up his house, and go more than twenty miles from his door just yet, but I was sure he would; he was working on it one step at a time. He was getting ready to give his radical yes to the life in front of him.

A radical yes is a mindset that can lead to personal assurance in the world. That yes can be seen in people who have confidence in a higher purpose that is beyond their own creating and in those who have conquered a radical individualism or even nihilism. The ways we gain that confidence or overcome that isolationist attitude often show us the creative powers that surge through life. Some call these powers God, and others see them as life itself. If we are willing to engage with uncertainty and to be changed, we may find spiritual awakening. Unitarian theologian James Luther Adams, in his essay "A Faith for the Free," writes, "The first tenet of the free person's faith is that our ultimate dependence for being and freedom is upon a creative power and upon processes not of our own making." Adams reminds his readers that we are created by, held in, and die into realities beyond our choosing. What we do in the circumstances of our lives teaches us about the deepest form of trust.

Our ability to give the radical yes to life usually grows by the experiences we have. Here is a story shared with me by a member of my church about a crucial moment in her life, when opening to the moment with a little attention and a radical yes made all the difference. She was attending a professional conference when she received a call telling her that her father was dying. When she arrived at his bedside she knew he didn't have long. Her other family members were rushing around, unaware of the precious moment before them or unable to attend to it. She told me,

I went to my father's bedside and stayed there. His eyes were closed and he was only semiconscious, mumbling something unintelligible. In the days when he was healthy, my father was never much for hugging or other displays of affection. As his health began to decline he softened and would always hug me hello and goodbye and occasionally tell me he loved me—something he'd never done before he got sick.

As I now sat down on his bed he reached for my hand. I couldn't tell if my father knew it was me; but he knew someone was there. I told him that I loved him and that he had been a good father to me and that it was okay for him to go, that everyone was there now and we'd be okay.

But apparently my father was going to die like he lived—on his terms, not mine. So I talked to him. And I talked and talked and talked. Then I ran out of things to say. Then we sat in silence together and listened to the various conversations going on around the room. The little room had about ten or twelve people in it. Occasionally my mother or an aunt would check in to see if dad was still breathing, and hospice took his vitals every thirty minutes. My brother would check on me and rub my shoulders or make sure I had something to drink. But otherwise, we were alone together in what seemed to be a jovial family gathering, and it really angered me. I didn't know what they all should be doing, but I was certain that this wasn't it.

As a way to calm myself and hopefully provide some comfort to my father, I began to recite a modified version of a loving-kindness meditation.

> May you be free from pain.
> May you be free from sadness.
> May you be free from suffering.
> May you be at peace.

I repeated it over and over as a sort of chant. Different family members would move in close to try to make out this strange thing I was chanting. But no one asked.

The mood in the room changed considerably when my father began crying out in pain. His breathing was labored. I began to synch my breath to his. This is what I would do during the moments when I wasn't talking, to let him know I was still there by his side.

Someone announced to the room that a tornado warning had been issued, and everyone except me and my two brothers left to move their cars to safety. Their cars? Really? I couldn't believe that while my father lay dying they were worried about their cars—more anger.

I was shocked and distraught to see how small and vulnerable my father looked. I was scared of losing my father. Scared of his pain. Scared of seeing him this vulnerable and helpless. Scared of watching him die. And scared that I wasn't doing this "right"—like there was some protocol that we should all be following and we weren't. I also realized that my family wasn't indifferent to what was occurring. They were all probably going through some similar emotional struggle. My anger vanished.

I acknowledged the fear and told my father that I was scared, that I didn't want him to die, but that I would be okay. That mom would be okay. That it would be hard, but we would get through it.

My father squeezed my hand. It may have been just a reflex; but I prefer to believe that it was my father letting me know that he knew I was there.

Then, as someone who left the Christian Church behind years ago, I did something that surprised me. I recited the Twenty-third Psalm.

As I said the last line of the psalm, my father opened his eyes, looked at my brother and me, and exhaled for the last time. It was one of the most intimate, powerful moments I have ever experienced.

I hadn't spoken the words of the Twenty-Third Psalm in over twenty years, since I left the Baptist church. I like to think that our presence and these words brought my dad some comfort in his final few minutes.

My brother and I stood up from my father's bed, hugged, and said, "I love you" through our tears. Then my brother said something I will carry with me forever. I remember it whenever I lose trust and begin to feel that I am not equal to whatever is before me. He said, "You did that exactly right."

I now trust that turning toward whatever is happening—no matter how scary or difficult or painful—is always a better path for me than running away or pretending that what is, isn't.

Finding ways to say yes rather than no can make all the difference. This kind of facing reality is also a form of building trust. Putting ourselves in tense and difficult situations in which we are challenged to do the "exactly right" thing can bring us great rewards. Running away, as my parishioner saw, is a worse option.

I aspire to the wisdom to know when that *yes* is imperative and when it can lead us astray. Saying yes is a tricky thing sometimes. Knowing our limits and what we can reasonably bear is something that comes with maturity. We often have to make mistakes with *yes* to learn those limits.

When I was just out of college, I applied for a teaching job with a program in Burlington, Vermont, for the most difficult students in the state. These were teenagers who had punched out their school principal, or worse. When I applied, the interviewer asked me if I had taught before. I said I had a degree in psychology and had been a counselor in a YMCA camp. I got the job and began teaching with a class of six students and two teachers. The classroom was always unpredictable. There were times when a student would come to class with stories of sleeping in cars because his home was too dangerous. Another time, the class got so out of control that during recess a student was found sitting in the basket on the basketball court, reciting a poem he had written. To say it was stressful would be to greatly understate what was going on there. Within months I developed life-threatening pneumonia, a severe tonsil infection, and a level of anxiety I had never felt before. I had said yes to a task I was not up for. I had said yes to a challenge without the maturity or experience to meet it. Now, as I look back on those difficult years in the classroom—struggling with stress-related vulnerability, and having to grow up quickly while still developing a sense of my own gifts—I wouldn't trade them for anything, but I paid the price. Whether we take a leap into something we aren't prepared for or go headlong into a project we have been preparing for all our lives, the price of saying yes to it can be balanced by the growth we gain.

The Buddhists talk about tuning ourselves like a musician tunes a string instrument: not too loose and not too tight. Too loose is never testing the limits of what we are capable of. Too tight is saying yes without regard for our safety. But the space between "too tight" and "too loose" challenges us appropriately, and is worthy of our faith explorations.

Reflection Questions

❧ On a scale of one to ten, how trusting do you think you are, in general?

❧ Can you surrender to something? What might that be?

❧ What are you willing to stop fighting with in your life?

❧ What must you give up to find a radical *yes* in the world?

❧ Can you say yes without knowing what will support you along the way?

❧ Write a list of what you trust and what you distrust. What can you learn from that list?

Loyalty

Before you begin a journey, you probably create a plan, make arrangements, call ahead, book tickets, and pack the things you need. If you are going on foot, you might buy a map or get a GPS unit, and check your equipment before you set off. Rarely do we walk out the door with no plan but to travel wherever the wind blows us. Indeed, we can become dedicated to our plans and the idea we have formed of the journey. This dedication is necessary to traveling, and the same dedication is necessary in life. But despite our plans, our journeys sometimes get detoured. In the same way, sometimes we make a commitment to the route we expect to take in life, and this commitment can blind us. Life occasionally takes us on unexpected paths. Both in travel and in life, there is something at play when we start off that can be described as loyalty or fidelity. By these words, I mean the commitments we make, the things that we care most deeply about, and our highest hopes.

In the 2016 Olympics in Rio de Janeiro, an amazing thing happened. In the opening ceremony's Parade of Nations, just before the representatives of the host country entered the stadium, a team of refugees walked in. For the first time in history, and in the midst of one of the largest refugee crises in the world's history, a team composed of people with no home—Ethiopians, South Sudanese, and Syrians displaced by war—was sponsored by the International Olympic Committee.

One member of this team was a young woman named Yusra Mardini. Her home in Damascus was destroyed in 2015 in the Syrian civil war, and she and her sister Sarah decided to flee. They went through Lebanon and then Turkey, where they paid to be smuggled into Greece. This was a time when thousands of migrants were dying in the Aegean Sea between Turkey and Greece. Horrifying images of drowned migrants were broadcast around the world. Mardini, her sister, and eighteen other migrants crowded into an inflatable dinghy for the crossing. But the dinghy's motor soon failed, and the boat began to take on water. Mardini, her sister, and another passenger jumped into the water and swam, pushing the boat, for more than three hours, until they reached the Greek island of Lesbos. Mardini's story and those of her teammates were well documented, and before she swam her first Olympic race they received a letter from Pope Francis that read,

I extend my greetings and wish you success at the Olympic Games in Rio—that your courage and strength find expression through the Olympic Games and serve as a cry for peace and solidarity. . . . Your experience serves as testimony and benefits us all. I pray for you and ask that you, please, do the same for me.

Mardini didn't medal in the Olympics, but she is a hero for her courage and, I would say, her fidelity. I use the term *fidelity* because she, her sister, and the third person who joined them did two things in the middle of the sea. They decided they could count on one another to help get everyone to their goal, and they didn't abandon the boat. They could have swum on together, leaving the doomed dinghy behind. But they felt a commitment to the others in the boat. They expressed a fidelity not only to familial ties but to their fellow travelers.

Faith can be described as fidelity. Traditionally, fidelity would be defined as faithfulness to God. But I think of it as a quality of loyalty or allegiance, a commitment of the self at the deepest level, or a pledge of the heart. Fidelity as faith is not faithfulness to statements about God, but a radical centering in the holy mystery of life itself.

I think of God as a notion we have of the numinous reality of a mystery beyond our comprehension. We could say that God is that which is beyond and within us. If we get stuck thinking of God as a supreme being who controls the universe and is entirely beyond our experience, we might miss the point that we are but a small drop in an ocean of life and are only here by a series of amazing accidents. That is enough mystery to keep me wondering about life. I don't like narrow definitions of God, which ask us to hand over all responsibility for our lives. I like to think that by seeing life as a miracle, we co-create existence. And this moves me to see faith as a way to have fidelity in life itself.

For the psychologist Erik Erikson, and also for many non-Christians, treating God as an object is very close to the idolatry that traditional religion warns against. Idolatry seems to me to be the opposite of faith. Idolatry hands over a good measure of responsibility to the thing or person being objectified and "idolized." Fidelity counterbalances idolatry. It requires that we put our attention beyond the things and people in our lives and on the highest purpose in life that we can conceive of. The founding fathers of our country expressed their fidelity in faith through their commitments to justice, truth, and the right of all to pursue happiness.

If we as a species are to survive, we may need to orient ourselves toward the triumph of good and compassion in the world. If this was the ultimate goal of humanity, which we pursued beyond our own individual lives, a lot of situations could be changed. Can we move from being oriented toward short-term gains to being oriented toward something larger than ourselves? Can we remain firm in our commitments to our families and friends while also seeing ourselves as being in service to something larger than them? These are age-old questions. Many have promoted the common good and pointed to our selfish natures. Buddhists have said our dis-ease in the world is caused by the many dimensions of desire that drive us on. Can we examine our impact on the world to balance the common good and the good of others with our personal gain? This dynamic is played out over and over in politics, economics, and everyday decisions. To fully invest in this kind of fidelity, we must consider what is most important to focus on, or to put it metaphorically, we might ask, "What is life's magnetic north?"

Ultimate commitments, or what theologian Paul Tillich calls "ultimate concern," pose a challenge to the spiritual life. Market forces push us to make our ultimate goals the goals of consumerism or greed. These cloud our decision making about things that will ground our spiritual lives. They prevent us from seeing the importance of other people and long-term goals that transcend wealth and accumulation. One reason I work in a church is that, ideally, everyone in a faith community works toward communal goals that guide how we make decisions and affect the larger world. Religions have always been about challenging human beings to live for ultimate loyalties that reflect a "holy" way of life. They usually center on ways to bring about and express love, respect, and justice for all, and rarely focus on personal gain and rank. This is what is so infuriating about prosperity theology in Christianity, which orients followers toward rewards in this life, such as wealth and property. Some religious movements—not all—have, to some degree, turned away from their original purpose and toward individual success. This is a warping of the values that guided their development, which focused on longer-term, more universal goals such as peace and the uplift of the poor. One reading of the Christian scriptures makes clear that personal gain in this life was not the goal of the early Christian communities.

Huston Smith, in *The Soul of Christianity*, writes, "Christian faith is not faith until it lives, moves, and has its being in the Christian performance known as discipleship. And it is not the work of individuals." Discipleship means commitment and a reorientation of one's life toward those highest goals. Many Christians have developed discipleship as an orientation of their actions toward God and in accordance with Jesus' teaching.

For non-Christians, discipleship might not be directed toward a person or God. Instead, it might ask us to prioritize and work toward helping others, to make justice, or to contribute to the common good. I have known people who could have closed their hearts and gone about their lives without a care for the world's concerns, but who instead became "disciples" to the cause of women or the poor. One friend had everything she could ever want but realized that if she didn't do something about the domestic abuse of women in her city she would feel complicit in it. So she spent much of her money to build and endow a women's shelter. And she didn't just stand back and wait for applause. She became an employee and spent hours helping women and families who came to the shelter to escape the terror in their homes. Her work is an example of what one Unitarian Universalist described to me as "commitment to each other and to the possibilities of what we can do together."

Unitarian theologian James Luther Adams provides some guidance here when he writes, in *The Prophethood of All Believers*, "The second tenet of the free person's faith is that the commanding, sustaining, transforming reality finds its richest focus in meaningful human history, in free, cooperative effort for the common good." This kind of discipleship means that we devote resources and energy to others' gain. Discipleship means commitment beyond lip service. It means living life with focus and direction.

I admit that my understanding of fidelity carries with it some level of judgment. But looked at through the faith lens, this judgment might be determined by asking yourself whether your "God" is too small. Are your loyalties self-serving, or do they serve some larger purpose? I would call any religious perspective that serves the self, without regard for the whole, a narrow faith.

Theologian Reinhold Niebuhr describes a "henotheistic faith" in his book *Radical Monotheism and Western Culture*. Niebuhr's understanding of henotheism is that it demands loyalty to one god as the priority over a multitude of gods that may have the same rank. In the modern understanding of this, according to Niebuhr, henotheism expresses itself in the exaltation of one social group to the exclusion of others, and examples of this include racism, nationalism, fascism, and communism.

For him henotheistic commitments are narrow because they are devoted to a single entity or aspect—whether God, career, or person—and they are ill-prepared for variety, complexity, and tragedy of human experience. In the face of tragedy, can such a faith help us to feel at home in the universe? If our fidelity is too small or self-serving, it could break and leave us as confused as kayakers in the fog.

Some parents have this kind of narrow faith. Instead of living side by side with their children and encouraging their development while pursuing their own purposes, they pour everything into their children, hovering over them at every turn, idolizing them, venerating them as gods, and thus missing the other people around them. They tend to act selfishly in service to their children. This leads to two problems. First, they forget that their children are living their own lives. Second, once their children break from their clutches, the parents are often left feeling heartbroken and empty.

I know one person who embodies a healthy form of loyalty. He is a Baptist, a dentist in a small town in Indiana, and he is committed to his town in a way I find rare in the world. He deliberately stayed in that town because of his family ties there, and because he wanted to be a small-town dentist serving not only his patients but also the poor. One day he realized that he couldn't treat all the people who came to his office needing assistance but were unable to pay for it. So he called around to other dentists in the area, secured a spot at the local Salvation Army, and built a dental clinic with donated equipment, staffed by volunteers. His commitment to building the common good in the town he grew up in was honorable. And he showed the same kind of fidelity to his friends. He told me that once he took a friend in and nursed him through the late stages of cancer. The friend died in the living room where we sat and talked. He even showed the same kind of fidelity to the land he owned in a small farming community outside of town. He described how he managed it carefully, learning to log it sustainably and deliberately, unlike the clear-cuts around the area.

I met this man on my solo bicycle journey. He took me in and cared for me with the same faith he practiced with his friends, family, and land. When he and his wife prayed for me during grace at breakfast on the day I left, I quietly wept from the feeling of being loved and cared for by almost complete strangers. That care came from the deep faith he and his wife possessed. This was not a faith in a God that would handle all my trials and tribulations, but a faith symbolized by their commitments to making the world a better place.

A member of my church once said to me, speaking metaphorically but with some passion, that she saw her purpose in life as raising her children well in order to improve the world. She said, "You are asking me about fidelity, but my devotion isn't to some God; it's to people and values. My highest commitment is to passing on improved DNA to my children, so they make the world a better place. Is there room for me in your model?"

This is a good challenge. It asks whether there is a hierarchy of commitment, of understandings of faith. Some would say so. Yet, an exclusive concern for and faithfulness to one's self or tribe can also reflect an unfaithfulness to the larger whole. For many generations we human beings have been too tribal. And smaller religious groups—like mine—seem to lack self-esteem. We Unitarian Universalists often commit our efforts to a local church without seeing the larger faith. We develop an allegiance to an individual or a small group, rather than to a larger effort. This can particularly result when we don't have a theological orientation that understands each person, church, and entity as serving a greater good. It can limit our fidelity to a higher purpose.

Whoever you are, you may benefit from exploring what is worth your larger commitment beyond your own care, tribal identity, or family. Asking yourself the reflection questions that follow may help get at the answer. The essential question is: What are you loyal to, and is it big enough? If you reflexively answer "yes" to the second part, it may be worth asking again.

Reflection Questions

❖ What loyalties do you cultivate? Do your loyalties hold your family or community together?

❖ What would friendship be without fidelity?

❖ What are you committed to with the fullness of your being?

❖ What are you ultimately loyal to?

Worldview

As a young Jewish boy living in western Massachusetts in the 1940s and 1950s, my father had vivid dreams of the young Dalai Lama. He dreamed that he was part of the Dalai Lama's court and spent time helping him. I imagine this was a way for my father to see the world he wanted to see. The Dalai Lama was in exile from his homeland, and my father was raised by Russian immigrants who had left everything to come to America. My father was also a child of the Second World War and grew up experiencing anti-Semitism so awful that he can hardly talk about it. It was natural for him to take refuge in an image of a peaceful existence with an ally who was teaching about compassion and wisdom. This image both arose from my father's worldview and painted the world he wished for. Sometimes the images of our dreams describe our view of the world better than we can in waking life. Sometimes they have profound effects on our lives.

Our worldview is how we compose meaning in the world and respond to it. The vision we have of the world pushes us to be honest with ourselves about how we see our lives, to have a "realistic" view of the world. This concept comes from the neorealist movement of the mid-twentieth century. Theologians like H. Richard Niebuhr wrote about worldview as an important aspect of living a spiritual life. In his book *The Responsible Self*, Niebuhr writes that how we see the whole of the world changes how we respond to it. A clearer understanding of the world requires sensitivity to both our beliefs and what we have decided to experience. How does our worldview affect our interpretation of what we see? When we encounter people and situations, what do our brains tell us? Why do different people see the same situation in different ways? In order to understand the concept of worldview, we must step back from our immediate reactions to things and ask why we react the way we do. To make this clearer, let me tell you about a friend.

My friend Mary, who lives in Covington, Kentucky, embodies how worldview affects our response to life with grace. She believes that hope is given to us and is part of us, and that we need to nourish it. She says that the extraordinary lives that we are given are vehicles to advance hope in the world, and that each of us, without exception, has a tremendous power to do extraordinary things. She describes this worldview by exclaiming with enthusiasm that we are amazing wonders and our wonderfulness can never be taken from us, that we are utterly loved by the world, and that

that love will go on and cannot be removed, no matter what situation we find ourselves in.

Acting on these understandings is her life's calling. Mary is a former Sister of Charity in the Catholic Church. Members of her former order devote themselves to works of charity through supporting education, caring for the sick, the aging, and the poor, and serving wherever there is a need. She left the order for many reasons, but especially because she felt it wasn't living up to its mission and it conflicted with her own broader worldview. She felt it oppressed people's spirits by setting people against each other rather than showing them the light that shines in each of us. The Church, she said to me, needs to move the love of humanity into the streets.

Mary is now a mother, grandmother, and teacher. Her worldview includes the idea that Christ is in the streets and in the sharing of hope with the poor. Once, when I was visiting her, she and I were on her front stoop, waiting on her husband before we went out for dinner. As we stood there, a man came by who looked homeless to me; he was disheveled and unkempt, and was collecting cans for deposit. He was Mary's neighbor, and she greeted him, repeating his name in a casual and loving way, holding his hand, and asking how he was doing and if he needed anything. She introduced him to me, and encouraged him with subtle and effective words. I have rarely seen this kind of gentle care given to a man on the streets. She loved him in that moment and gave him a sense of purpose in that brief exchange. Her approach was kind and gentle, and she affirmed his humanity in a special and honest way, as I am sure few others would whom he might encounter that day. For her, Christ was in her neighbor, and in their moment together she greeted the Christ in him.

Mary's worldview is that we all need to invest hope in every human being we meet, and that we meet Christ in the poor. She learned this, she told me, from her mother, who was a living example of how someone understands and acts on a worldview. She learned as a child how to be a daughter of charity, to love people and especially the poor. She recalled to me an early awareness of the people on the streets in Baltimore and wondering, "Where are they going? Why are they by themselves?" And she told me that their loneliness connected to her loneliness, and their humanity met hers. Her worldview took shape in those moments of asking questions and observing the world as a young child, and it continues to develop through her love of those around her. In these ways there is coherence between how Mary sees the world and what she does with her life. She is not a Sister of Charity anymore, but she is a charitable person in all ways, and without effort she practices her worldview on the streets of Covington and everywhere she goes.

Each of us might structure our worldview in different ways. My father saw a world in need of compassion and wisdom, and followed that path to Buddhism as an adult. Mary saw a world in need of hope and charity, and followed that view to a life of small yet important acts of love. I once met three young adults in Vermont who were interns on an organic farm, growing vegetables to be cooperatively distributed at a fair price to their community. These young adults saw a world that held a population so large they understood that even the highest levels of education guaranteed nothing. They told me their friends had worldviews that ranged from questioning their parents' assumption that hard work would yield rewards to expecting revolution and the collapse of the energy infrastructure. They were seeking alternative ways to carve out a corner of the world for themselves, ways that would be sustainable and contribute to the community.

Worldviews are valid and important to listen to and learn from. They have many dimensions and are changed by events and experiences, and because of this they can vary between generations. People have said to me that some experiences are within our control and others are not, and their outcomes can affect our visions of the world. This is absolutely true. Both personal experiences and world events can change our worldview, sometimes for the better and sometimes not. Anyone who lived through one of the genocides of the twentieth century might react to that experience by composing a worldview that sees the universe as evil. But it is also possible for someone who has lived through horrific experiences to see the world in other ways. It may be true that how we are wired has an effect on this in ways we are not prepared to understand.

When I was a child, I met a man who had survived the Holocaust, and he helped shape my view of the world. He lived in my hometown. The Nazis had taken him and his father to a concentration camp because they were Jews. He slaved away in a labor unit, was beaten by Nazi and Jewish guards, and was made to eat food mixed with the blood of other prisoners who had dared question the servers in the food line and been beaten with the serving spoons, sometimes to death. Eventually he escaped the camp with the aid of some good townspeople who came to the camp to bring provisions. This man should have seen the world as evil and unredeemable. But he didn't. He had become a teacher, and in retirement he spent his time visiting classrooms in my hometown and telling his stories. He believed that we students needed to know what had happened in the Holocaust, and he hoped that we might see some glimmers of the hope he saw in the world and believe with him in the redemptive power of doing the right thing. He believed strongly, as I do, that good triumphs over evil in the end. Perhaps this cheerful man in part influences my worldview. Whenever I think about war and other horrible things we humans do to one another, I see his smile and hear him telling us that we are good. I carry the echo of his voice with me. It echoes in my life because a man who overcame the temptation to give up on the world passed on to children a new worldview, different than they could ever imagine.

There are many models for encountering the world, maybe as many as there are people. Those who came out of concentration camps seeing the world as unredeemable probably lost all hope. Those who took a negative view of the world in all aspects of their lives probably didn't spend time teaching children about the things they encountered or the ways they found to survive. People with negative worldviews often fail at making real connections with others, and this failure can lead them to nihilism or to accepting forces of oppression, indignity, and even violence. I suspect that modern terrorism is driven by giving up on the world and seeing it only in light of its failings.

Christianity has traditionally argued that a worldview can take one of three stances: the world or universe is essentially evil, indifferent, or lifegiving. This means that we have to think about God's creation, everything from amoebas to solar systems, and form an opinion on it. If we see it as evil, we have to fear everything around us, including God. An evil world requires forces of good to counteract the evildoers. It requires us to protect ourselves from corrupting elements. Those who see the world as essentially evil rely on force in responding to it, and probably live by rigid rules. Theologically, they might reject ambiguous religious statements in favor of concrete ones. And, whether or not they are religious, they may promote a type of adherence to the way they see the world, preventing the possibility of broad interpretations and a diversity of opinions.

The second possibility is to see the universe and its movements as essentially indifferent. This view says that neither amoebas nor solar systems nor anything else has any goal or purpose. Seeing what happens to us and the shape of our lives as purposeless might mean throwing up our hands and concluding that the world is awash in chaos, and little should—or can—be done about it. This view too can lead to nihilism. If creation is indifferent, and so is God, then life might have little purpose. This worldview is similar to a secular, "unbelieving" view. On the other hand, it might also be true that an indifferent world needs our attention; that even if the purpose of the world is unclear, we, as the consciousness of the world, can be clear about our purpose. This view might lead us to conclude that whether the world has an inherent purpose or not, we human beings can give it intention and make it bend toward such goals as justice and peace. Most progressive religious people take this view.

The third possibility, in the Christian model, is to see the world as essentially lifegiving and nourishing, filled with responsibility and grace. This option will likely guide us to a sense that a purpose or plan exists, and urge us to feel a responsibility to carry it out. This worldview encourages the Christian faithful to take seriously the stewardship of the world's gifts. Seeing creation, including ourselves, as a gift with an essential purpose can prompt the faithful to strive to actively discern the plan and their own parts in the whole, and to reflect on what it means to encounter evil or indifference. On the other hand, a belief in an ultimate plan or purpose can also be used to coerce others.

Here is a story of two women who were working together who had differing worldviews. Elie, a sixty-something, educated, intelligent woman, lived in rural Vermont. She came from a Jewish family and had married a Jewish man, but she called herself only "culturally Jewish," meaning that she lit Sabbath candles a few times a year and held Passover seders with her friends when possible. She had a lot of questions about why people would be religious or need a religious community, since she did not. Nor did she did see herself as spiritual, although the family rituals of gratitude at the dinner table she described to me and the tie she felt to nature sounded spiritual to me.

Elie told me that she had been a community organizer in New Hampshire. Her work grew out of her moral stance that justice was important, and out of her belief that humanity was essentially good and we had to work for each other rather than ourselves. But she had a coworker who was a devout Catholic, and who did the same work because of her faith. Elie couldn't see why her coworker would do this work out of an obligation to her Catholicism, and the other woman couldn't see how Elie could do it without a religious framework. And yet both Elie and her colleague were acting out their faiths. Her Catholic colleague responded to the biblical obligations to clothe and feed the poor, to see Christ in the poor, and to be God's servant wherever she was called to confront injustice. And Elie's moral imperative was a deep faith in the goodness of humanity and the potential to transform the world.

Why did each woman fail to see that a faith dimension existed in the other? I think we are often so blinded by our traditional ideas of faith that we can't shift the paradigm to include those who express faith in different ways. Elie might not have understood why someone would need the models set forth in a religious tradition to do justice work because she herself had rejected traditional religious language and structure. Similarly, her colleague failed to see Elie's deep loyalty to humanity and her trust in it to do the right thing and try to improve the world as a kind of faith because her beliefs lacked a traditional religious structure.

In my view, both of these women had genuinely faith-based reasons for the work they did. And both might have profited from trying to understand the other's worldview. That exchange of understandings could have furthered their self-discovery and helped break down the walls that kept them from seeing each other fully. Despite the respect and friendship they shared in the work they did together, they were in some ways blocked by their definitions of faith and spirituality, and most importantly by their different views of the world.

Diversity in worldviews is not just important but essential, as long as we can talk with one another about our differences. In order to do this, we must identify our own perspectives. If we can do that, we can create some guidelines by which to judge our actions and ourselves. There are as many worldviews as there are people and each of us lives with challenges and influences that shape us. It is a mistake to judge the worldviews of others without considering how they may have come to be; doing so means we will miss important factors in all our discussions.

As we experience life, we also experience change. It is good to be willing to challenge ourselves and ask hard questions about why we see the world the way we do. The answers will determine how we respond to the world and compose meaning in it. How we see the world affects what religion and faith path we pursue and how we conduct our lives. We explore our visions of the world not in order to judge one view as better than another, but to understand what actions might result from our worldview, what has lived and died in us as a result of our experiences, and what we want to nurture for the future.

The biblical book Ecclesiastes has a well-known passage, later turned into a folk song, that declares "for everything there is a season." We read it so often at memorial services because we want to juxtapose life and death and everything that happens in between. Whether we believe God places us in the mix of human life or we believe we are passing on DNA as travelers in this human journey, we know that the one constant in life is change. In her poem "To Fill the Void," Mary Zoll explores how faith, of whatever kind, is informed by the knowledge of our own mortality.

I do not care if your true god controls
the whole sweet universe or just your own
small piece of it. Your god may fit black holes
and worms in some grand scheme and rule alone
or with a multitude of jealous gods
or spirits of wild animals and trees.
This god may want you sacrificed, or awed
by sacred myths, or praying on your knees.
That god may let you meditate or smoke
cigars and twirl around. You may prefer
a god or goddess, think it's all a joke—
there is no god, just science, cold and pure.
Just tell me you belong, your faith's enough
to let you sleep at night, despite sure death.

Part of being honest with ourselves is to confront the fact that there will be a time to die. Knowing that both shapes and is shaped by our worldview. It matters what happens to us, what we learn, and how we look at the world because who we are is made up by our response to the worldview we develop.

Reflection Questions

❧ What vision of the world do you carry? What influences have helped shape your vision?

❧ Who has modeled a vision you kindle in your life? How has your vision changed?

❧ How does your vision influence your actions, especially your behavior toward others? Is there coherence between your vision and your actions?

Becoming Faithful

In the mountains far north of Katmandu, just five kilometers from the Tibetan border, I'm sitting on a rock the size of an elephant, deep in contemplation.

No, I'm not pondering the meaning of life. I'm concentrating on a much more practical question. Should I continue on my quest, following the yak herder trails? Should I wait here and continue pondering my decision? Or is it time to turn back and say, "I gave it my best"?

I'm sitting on this rock as part of my pursuit of enlightenment. I am twenty-two years old, and I am in a part of the world famous for those seeking the same lofty goal. Facing the unpredictable weather, hiking in silence, camping, and keeping a journal—these, I felt, were the necessary elements of a journey to elevate my consciousness.

I was with a friend, an avid New England hiker, now stricken with dysentery. We had been traveling for eight days, schlepping our tent, cook stove, and other essentials for survival in a climate known to challenge the best of adventurers. And after having climbed to this mountain valley, I fell into an exhausted sleep.

I awoke to a foot of fresh snow, as if the universe were playing with me by piling on yet another challenge. The tent was wet, the trail invisible, and the only sounds were the tinkling of a tiny brook and the ever-present symphony of wind.

Had there been a warning in the giggling of the three monks we had met the day before, when we told them of our journey? They were hard to take seriously.

They lived in a circular white shrine known as a *stupa*, divided into small, cluttered rooms. We stepped inside and were introduced to the abbot, who sat fingering his beads as he read through ancient Buddhist texts. We had brought special Buddhist threads blessed by the Dalai Lama with us as offerings to the monks in exchange for advice. The monks received the threads with surprise and then shared a spare lunch with us of watery barley stew and salted butter tea. We had pointed to our destination, the plateau above them, at an elevation of fourteen thousand feet, and their laughter had accompanied our departure. Now a day later we were sitting on a rock, asking questions and wondering what was next.

We had set off with the goal of climbing Himalayan peaks and retreating into the quietest parts of the earth. We thought of ourselves as modern-day monks in the tradition of

Basho, a seventeenth-century Zen Buddhist who hiked the length of Japan as a spiritual quest. He wrote haiku about his journey, including this gorgeous piece that describes his enjoyment of the mountain blooms:

Traveling this high
mountain trail, delighted
by violets

And, we could have written this one in the Langtang Valley:

An autumn wind
More white
Than the rocks in the rocky mountain.

We remembered and read Basho that morning when we woke to the snow. The weather's challenges were only a small part of my difficulties; I also struggled with our gear and my friend's fears. We decided, before we took any action, to sit in meditation on a large rock and wait for the silence to speak to us. Should we go on into the mountains where we could live and meditate, or not? Little did I know that the response I would receive would change my life.

Up on top of that Himalayan mountain, with the storm in the distance and my sick friend asking whether we should press on or turn back, I heard an answer to my question, the kind that comes rarely in life. The words I heard as I sat on the edge of the world were "Return home, and serve your people."

I realized that I couldn't stay there, searching for my personal enlightenment. I had to descend and go back to my life. Faith work requires both the climb up and the descent from the mountain. The journey, our soulful search for meaning, must always return us to engagement and action.

If we pay attention, we will realize that we are all on a journey to understand the urgings of our lives. Some of those journeys take us to the edge of the world, and some take us to the kitchen sink, where we do the dishes. The answer I received in that mountain range was a call to a personal faith; an internal force asked me to take life seriously, dig into my soul to find what treasures were yet undiscovered there, and know that my life had a purpose.

Such insights don't always come to us as clearly as a call to faith on a mountaintop. They are often clouded by our desires and confusions. But they come all the same, and they define our faithful responses to the world. They may not demand that we obey traditional authority or dogmas, only that we pay more attention to what is happening around us.

Humans are unique in that we seek meaning in our lives rather than just working to survive. Look at the prevalence of self-help books, prayer groups, the teachings of gurus, and lectures designed to allay our fears about existential issues of life and death. We are meaning makers. We might even say that making meaning is our job in the universe.

Just as important as knowing what faith looks like is accepting that this knowledge must lead to action so that our faith continues to grow. Answering faith-centered questions and bringing together what we say we know about ourselves leads us to put our values into action. George Marshall, in his book *The Challenge of a Liberal Faith*, writes, "To live religiously is the prophetic risk for [us all]. It means to live as though there are values in life, that we will create through experience the arena for expressing those values. It means we have a faith that shines through life."

Who do you know who has a faith that shines through life? I can think of many historical figures, from Henry David Thoreau, who went to the woods to "live deliberately," to activists who work to save our planet, who call on us to unite faith and action. Martin Luther King Jr. is such a figure, as is Sister Joan Chittister, a Catholic nun who works for equality and has a fierce feminist faith she employs to challenge the Catholic Church.

I once scoffed at Julia Hill, a young woman who had climbed up into an ancient redwood tree in California and spent years living in its branches to save it from loggers. Now I see this as an amazingly heroic act uniting belief with the other aspects of her faith. I am sure she didn't stay in the tree for so long without some reflection, and she concluded that life matters, the earth matters, and what we do with our lives matters. Maybe the end result of reflecting on faith is the ability to live deliberately and allow our values to guide our actions. To live in a way that is coherent with what is calling us within is the goal of life, and ultimately an act of faith.

As I sat on the Himalayan rock so many years ago, I got a glimmer of what I was supposed to do as a faithful person. The personal faith I could connect with demanded that I look at life earnestly, that I respond to the callings and urgings of the deepest places of my spirit, and that I understand that we each make meaning with the lives we lead, whether we are a twenty-two-year-old seeker, a grandmother in a poor city in Kentucky, or a dentist who commits to his community. Each of us can give back to this needy world just by knowing ourselves a little better.

As we near the end of this journey, look back at your responses to the questions I have asked throughout the book. Or go back and answer them again, now that we have come this far. Use what the Zen monks call "beginner's mind," a mind that is open to surprises and challenges. Look for patterns or places where that feeling of being stuck resides. See what changes are crying out to be made, what explorations are calling, and who else needs to be part of this faith discussion. All mountain climbers know that, once they reach the top, they must come down; there will be more mountains to climb. A faith perspective is one that remains open to change, shuns the fixity of dogmatic perspectives, and is able to remain vulnerable, trusting that change happens.

While writing this, I looked out a window onto a tree farm and a small reflective pond in Vermont. I thought of the four panes of a window as a metaphor for a way to compose a faith—through guiding beliefs, areas of trust, loyalties, and worldview. On the other side of these panes is a landscape, and that landscape is the wholeness of one's faith. The panes of the metaphorical window are made up of the experiences we have had and all we have learned. We may see the pond and the trees easily enough, but it takes time to take in the whole landscape. That larger view is what I wish for you.

I hope that we are the people the world needs. The world does not ask whether we "have faith" or "don't have faith." Such a binary perspective is limiting, divisive, and at some level abusive. The question I am asking is: What type of faith is possible? By doing this faith work we can become less calculating and more wise, less critical and more inviting, less divided and more loving. If we delve deeply enough into this work, we will approach each other as people of faith, in the way the world's religions intend us to: impelled by love and compassion, seeing each other with open eyes, and finding that cooperation toward the benefit of everyone is the ultimate goal that tugs at the heart of us all.

Reflecting on things of the soul rarely leads to destructiveness. Many people do destructive things in the name of faith, but I believe that this is a distortion of the meaning of faith. Rote dogmatic enactment of any faith can be dishonest. This is why I am asking those who delve into faith work to approach it with a sense of doubt, understanding that their initial answers will not necessarily be their final ones, and reflecting on and answering the urgings of the soul. I am asking you to see more than one way toward faith, to embrace a complexity that will lead you to a lifelong deepening.

Whether we are deeply religious or not religiously affiliated at all, we can all be faithful. The key question to consider is: Can we live our lives from a spiritual perspective in a way that does more good than harm in the world? All religions have tried to ask this of us, but many have been corrupted by dogmas that strayed from the religion's essence. We are all travelers, walking many paths through our lives. How we walk them makes all the difference. Be warned: Answering the questions I have posed in this book is risky. If you take the questions and the answers you find to heart, they may change your life forever.

I ask you to examine your faith and develop it so that it is not stagnant, controlled by creeds, or owned by a few, but is your living, breathing, personal perspective. Each person's answers to the questions in these chapters are undoubtedly different from everyone else's. But in reflecting on the questions together, we can contemplate who we are, pushing aside the temptation to limit our worldviews to the destructive binaries of win/lose and either/or. We can all be faithful. Being faithful expands us all.

Up in the Himalayan mountains, with the storm in the distance and my sick friend asking whether we should press on or turn back, I learned the purpose of my life. The words "Return home, and serve your people" have guided my actions ever since. Down from that mountain, past the monastery with the giggling monks, through villages and cities and miles of adventures, I have been trying every day to return home to myself and to answer that calling. I have been trying to live a life that serves my people. This has required me to reflect deeply about what service means and who my people are. In the end the mountain was where all my questions met a single sentence answer and at that time it was enough. I'm not saying we will all have such moments. In fact, I think I needed such a dramatic answer to my question, in such a dramatic setting, because I was so thickheaded that I couldn't hear it while sitting at home with my family or walking the paths of my neighborhood.

I have never gained much by staying home; adventure, whether through the world or the spirit, has fed my soul. I hope these tales have fed yours, and that you hear your answers right where you are. Perhaps the climb we have taken in the pages of this book is all the start you need. My friend

Ed, who lives in New York's Catskill Mountains, once told me, "The cynic is the one who has never experienced the richness of the world." Ed got it right. The richness of our world feeds our inner lives, changes who we are, and opens us to possibility. And that richness is available to all who seek it. Good luck and good wishes on your journey. Now it is time to face your mountain!

Reflection Questions

༂ Now that you have read this book and contemplated the questions it asks, what does your faith look like?

༂ What do the journeys of your life tell you about how you have composed your faith?

༂ Does faith mean something different to you now?

༂ What would the world be like if we could see through the four windowpanes clearly?

Acknowledgments

I would like to thank my family for their patience, encouragement, and concern through all the adventures and time given to create this book. Thanks especially to Rori Kanter for long conversations that led to the ideas in the book and for being a lifelong writing collaborator. This project could not have come together without the support of First Unitarian Church of Dallas and the sabbatical time granted to me to write about and reflect on my faith and ministry. A few friends kept me going during the depth of the writing phase: Ray, Sarah, and Audrey at Square Deal Farm, who nourished me with tacos and time for fun and hikes between writing sessions in Vermont. Thanks to Charles Vorkoper and Carolyn Smith-Morris, Bill Barnett, Aaron White, Tracy McShan, John Buehrens, Robert Stock, and Pam Lange for all the good advice they gave during the writing and editing process. And thanks to all the Unitarian Universalist churches surveyed in the initial study that led to my dissertation on faith. I am grateful to Rebecca Parker,

Earl Holt, and Carl Scovel for being intellectual and ministerial mentors to me for the last twenty-five years. Thank you to all those who took me in on my cross-country bicycle trip, especially Mary and Rick Hulefeld and Ed the Oracle of the Catskills. Some of those who hosted me on my trip have not been named to protect their privacy. Finally, much appreciation goes to Dr. Ruben Habito and Dr. Fred Schmidt, who guided my doctoral thesis process at Perkins Theological School, which led to this book. And thanks to Marshall Hawkins and the staff at Skinner House Books for pulling me along!